Valjeane Olenn
from Hugh
Xmas '81

By Larry Woiwode

What I'm Going to Do, I Think, A NOVEL (1969)

Beyond the Bedroom Wall, A NOVEL (1975)

Even Tide, POEMS (1977)

EVEN TIDE

FARRAR

STRAUS

GIROUX

NEW YORK

EVEN TIDE
by Larry Woiwode

for Carole

VALENTINE'S DAY, 1971

EVEN TIDE

Done.
Schemes, lies,
Half-love,
The rose,
Both red and white,
The rugged cross rotting,
The rude
Intransigent
Jokes I made of myself:
Bum,
Prodigal son
To anyone
Older who praises me;
Junk collector,
Jealous husband,
Drunk,
Blue head burning blue
Ohios in the night;
My sempiternal tune
For some
The time a match head
Flares,
Ba-ba bum,
Drum and decorum,

Watch it,
I've—

Oh, say, do you have a match?

ONE

1

Who's presumed upon this tree?
What knife can say "I love you"?

2

Red-gold glowing low in a chalice,
A heaving engine dieseling over out of phase
And then not, dying driving, Kathumpa, thumpa
Thum. Gold hair flays, flays, flays our faces
In your absorption to envelop up above.

"Am I woman? *Half* woman? Am I *me*?" I whine,
As you transfix a new axis, galaxied.
"Which planet would you care to stop at?
This one?" *No, No,* you say, and I'm
Submerged in the outpour of Earth's shining sea.

3

In winding seaward on the wind
The light free thoughts of a man alone
Mingle with other filled winds gathering moisture
Over canyons, pastures, tree-geysering hills, the bone

Of a highway knitted by a bridge
That arches over one bound but active stream
That curls across shelves of upper continent to a river
That meets the entering sea—fit vault for the undisclosed schemes

And lost scales and shed skins and all the cut-free thoughts of
Young men alone, living out their apprenticeships in faithless love.

4

The mountainous spires of consciousness,
The ocean beneath plunging up in its flues,
The isthmuses in the vista beyond, the mist,
All bound within the word-barrel of one skull,
Seeing itself in ferment alone in its one dream.

Should I do as others do and rise?
I do and break the morning open with my eyes.

Then drown the best words in wine
And drugs (legal ones, mostly, no less,
From the local pharmacy) and sleep,
And see them return in an altered
State, wild-eyed, condemning beasts,
Syllables giving a hacksaw rattle,
Vowels and claws going for my throat,
And unless I accept them then they
Bolt away, wise to false perfection,
As bitter and amazed as the cat
I couldn't get to drown at about eleven;

As once at the airport when I let you
Walk by, light-haired lady of the lakes,
Looking so hard for who I expected to see

I overlooked you, and you stepped up with
Your hair in a new style, the height of it,
A blaze of white hat around your face, you
Whispering, "I'm here; ah, hey, you, it's *me*,"
And I cried, "My God, you look like Lady Brett,"
You merely opened your eyes in a wider parabola
And said: "Well, this is New York, isn't it?
This was how I was sure you expected me to be."

O *La Fleur* of the glacial lakes and streams, so right;
Your convex shape of illumination, my dread of night.

The stars spinning within their proscribed swings,
My mind loose and apocalyptic again, treading
The dead line between being loved and cursed,
So alive with both I want to burrow into
The fur of my mother, who left first.

5

Horses sleep in the wind-driven snow northwest
Out of Fargo. Flocks of buntings come down in
Swirls of flakes into fields of stalks. Night
Appears an hour ahead this early March. Thick
Flakes darken and slow. Slush forms on the horses'
Backs. They shudder it free, steam, are cold once
More, stomp, let it build up. No colors now show.
Great heads droop toward drifts climbing up dark
Hocks as silence ferries in its crystalline blow:
Out of Fargo, apart from you across a curve of
Continent this season, seeing snow fall
Over these of all the sleeping horses in between.

6

A load of grain,
Wheat heavy in a huge
Wagon, pneumatic strain
Of tires flattened on the grass;

Beside a pile
Of cinders carried here in a coal bucket,
In a while
Scattered ash, stands a wagon

Heaped with a mine
Of the beaded fire that we, years younger,
With the help of wine,
Pulled from there to the insides of one another.

7

I have no protectorate but porous skin
Which sheathes my flesh and lets it sweat at will
But allows abuse and influence to enter in
Without discrimination, where it faces a slow
And goatish mind going in girlish rotations. *Hmm,*
What can I fashion out of this sheet of tin?

Backstage thunder with the voice of a naked god?
A rumbling cross to flounder with? A wobbly sword?
Something more fireproof than a box of leaves,
More deflective than flesh, those nights in *amour,*
But not as a shield, scraps of which could be
Used, perhaps, to patch the worst of the wounds

While they healed—   Ah: a
Gray-blue mailbox. It reads, *Woiwode's Woven Screens.*

TWO

for Eugene

This is in the form of a pause
Or personal witness
For you with eyes on these:
    When I think of the trees
I've knocked down,
I'm still and uneasy,
And it doesn't help to have seen
Beaver fell more birches
Along a single backwoods stream
In one spring than this book
Will touch, or doesn't me;
So if you would write
Whatever you'd like
And wherever you please
On these wide white pages,
I'd feel less restless,
Destructive, detached,
Less guilty and temporal,
A bit more at ease, perhaps,
That my work as a servant,
Just begun, has joined hands,
And in most cases much better,
                    Sincerely.

8

You expect these lines to come easy?
Or be chaste? This isn't prose, milady,
Not for me, but from me. The wind stills,
Snow hangs in crystals from the tree limb,
Repeating that individual sun overhead,
And I have to reconstruct our way
Through glints
Of semaphore
With lines and
Seismographs,
When actually it overcame us so easily.

9

The days I see through have turned surreal;
Images rise of their own volition
On spiderlike legs
And crawl across my vision asleep or at this;
All that's been sustaining me is cottage cheese and my bent
(Is it true that true illumination is bed partner to insanity?)
To sit all night and into the day,
Borne on this rickety chair
Through the richness of the past
(Yes, I still have my typing job, I say, when you dare ask),
Knowing one more row will be done for a—

Then I'm given a vision of the broad swath
I've cut over your half
Of our world
All these years, those miles,
And see my job
Go up
Without a shock
To warn,
Outside hardly a sheaf.

10

Why wade?
Wit whoa, Didi?
Witty Whitey
Wee wood
Woe weed
A whee ah
Wide weighed wad
(And rhyming with load)
Ah woda wode?
Would you could if you wanted to be?
That's your signature?
(Billowy clouds above a ragged sea above which is a tipped mast.)
What do you do? No,
I won't take a personal check.

Oh.
Well, it's wí-wood-e (with an ending long E)
In the family's pronunciation, that word;
You've robbed me of the syllable of
Antiquity,
The horses' hooves at a gallop, the flashing
Axes, the night stamp that makes the name home for me. Woiwode.
You'd be as surprised as I, I bet, sir, to see that in Webster's Third.

11

My blackened eye turns upon zero,
My good eye turns on "Good night,"
Here in the depth of December
Where we're locked within light.

My left hand reaches for zero,
My right hand scratches in the night
In the light of a lantern, December
Light, locked within light.

My right leg is the pole zero,
My left leg stumps in unequal height
Around it around through December
In this lockstep within light.

My right mind rejects the sum zero,
My mind that's left is all right,
As this month, December, your month,
I enter you with no right.

12

A shaggy chrysanthemum, clumsy flower, like the pinwheel
That spun on its stick at Coney Island, raggedly humming *Mine*.
Yours beside it. Wind.
Both motionless, rolled-back petals crushed up against a spine
Pricked by a pin.
Between their whitish stare, a broad leaf's a spire
Against the pale blue of the wall, a place for the eye
To reconnoiter. The plastic pitcher you use,
Freckled with copper-metallic flakes, translucent,
Tall, intended to contain
The transformation
You aspire to, appears to open
Along its length and lets leaves
Spill down toward your parting hand;
They're held away from the dresser top,
The floor, by three pinkish wild-rose
Knots (no, four) and clinging ferns
That tremble from your strings and
Skeins of distinction, where,
Between a pair of buds, and
In spite of them, air
Pirouettes
(You rise to this occasion),
And is stabbed through wire with a stem.

13

Are there quail in the state where you are now,
In that barren state you've traveled to
To move from the shadow my stone love
Cast, are there quail there?

They drum from the brush as I walk at night
And I can see with their sound the way
You'd undo and let your hair fall as
It fell ("It falls like a quail
That's hit," you wrote)
From the unmoving mastery of your night face.

Now, at night, it settles for me into the most
Venal of thoughts; this one I tricked,
You I could have loved, perhaps,
A half dozen laid. Forgive me.

Forgive *me.*

I do, with light breaking in on your map.

Forgive me.

14

Clouds rib the air of memory,
Dreams invade the sky;
Your arrival, rain.

Tilted from sheets,
Water leans into the dream
And flows through a hole to me.

Bound in this caricature, lady,
You reach to me and paper tears,
Planes of light eclipse your arm,

Rapids scatter over the day's edge,
Bringing me nearer that redundant sea,
And your good red blood, knocked from its hold

A week ahead, spots the floor as you walk away from me.

THREE

15

Fall rain at four in the afternoon.
We put away brushes and cans of stain
And come indoors. Flaying nature waits
Around us in the half-done lodge, at this wooded
Bluff's edge, where beasts and I can smell your blues.

Scattered pools lift up gold in
The low sunlight; gold leaves drift
And drip from the hornbeam, the maple,
The beech; a robin does a skating run on
The rainy grass and *Me? Me?* his eye on me repeats.

I clamp my hands between my thighs
To keep them still, or else polish a stone—
"With the patience of Job," I later write, and boil—
Until its charcoal fossils flume beneath an apparent
Transparency: hexagonal bays bound by bonelike white streams.

In Williamstown, in another state
And time, sealed in temporary British rooms, flat
In bed, I listened for noises at six until my listening
Summoned up a creaking man in formal clothes, outlined in neon,
Who gave off green. A full week to write you even this little bit of
It, Bill; a cold spoon on the birthright of speech, it seems . . . Predestiny.

The sun. I wirebrush each inch of outside
Area left exposed, brush on brown creosote stain, and see it
Soak deeper than water into these drying logs, unaware that I
Was ever of importance in an earnest scheme, or as handsome as I
Was that season, as this snapshot might help prove, as surely beautiful as
I was that fall, then, rising from her into You, you, and *you*. I mean . . .

16

A butterfly left by my left ear
In the light way that memory goes,
And now a dozen bushes of untrimmed
Roses (sorry, Bill) just fell from my nose.

Here comes the Baptist Church Road
Great Blue Heron, those three crows,
Now another butterfly, mimicking a marigold,
And then the flurry for your disappearance (by
Wings, wisdom—which?), but you stay like a rooted stone.

So I realize that this is merely dross
I must get rid of, and that I've grown again
To accommodate your trust, as Brook and I, later
Cawing like two lookouts through the trees, tried to
Signal across the valleying darknesses to you at the bonfire, the newborn
There, and our four living and dead mothers around you in moth-filled air.

17

That butterfly's going after a ball of light, or
The sun of my son's preying across your lawn,
Beating his wings in a double reflection.

Or is he that form that follows in the
Shape of a shadow? Called, Nathaniel, I'd
Fly to your realm and shield you from sight, I,
Your father, who never saw you alive in this life.

O a lost song, *bitte*, wee.

I come from my parents' thighs,
    My voice is small.
    Each day I crawl
From task to task, an unvoiced cry
    The shape of a swan,
    Violet-colored, at
    The base of my lungs,

Mute. But as evening comes it
    Grows to the hoot
    Of an owl, a "Whoo?"
To the nodding swan, who replies,
    "I by nature am quiet
    As my parents' thighs,
    Having no tongue."

18

I am the thorn cut by you along with
    The red rose.
And who can say, once staked in white sun,
    Which of us chose

It? It's true you eye me just like the rose.
    Is it from
The mazes I excite when I socket the bone
    Of your thumb?

As you dream of blood, old slaughterhouses,
    And of how you conspire
With me to make most women trust mounting
    Martyrdom's spire,

Man, red rose, bloody bloom of full-blown
    Flyblown desire,
Strung from great Christ's spiked gardenia along
    Singing barbed wire.

19

Do you navigate over pastures of beasts,
Over seas of swirling plankton in grief
With your blossom still unopened in its pack?
When you were alive, when you were twenty,
Were the five glowing spheres in your body,
These five adults now ranging over their fields,
Chosen to follow from threshold and state to state
To continent to repeat your falling rite in the way
You arrive at a glide in this album next to
Where the Polaroid of *Her Asleep* lies on the bed
Beside her asleep? Do you hear all five—
Do you hear all six cry out, *Come back! Come back!*

20

When coffins float in their own silk ocean
And rose waves erode a dock of wreaths,
I hope I'm up to help roll that rock back from
The blinding justice of the sky's great—

I of necessity hold low tray soul;
It's mostly heart and bleeding, Jesus.
Gentlemen, be generous, clabber me up in your
Rolls and let the commoners do the eating.
You see, I've come from across the sea
Families and families ago, and I feel it.
One of those fellows sold a good heart for his
Threepenny soul. See uncles, aunts, Norwegians,
Nieces, Germans, Finns, English, and some Scots,
Plus a trainload of cousins and their daughters
And sons you'll never count winding away out
Of sight down and through a coulee, a few of
Whom'll watch for my words to fly away or whoa,
Have seen me on a hot horse without a saddle,
And know
About the pieces
Of silver in my three—

Hey, I'm the white cat that laid that hash on you

In Red Wing, Minnesota, black troubadour back from Hawaii,
And now I need a tune or two to help ease my blue-edged,
Bruised, indebted, and undoubting—

I mean,
The many times I've pried across
The flyways
Into which
The past leads
(she ain't heavy-
vee,
she ma
ma-ah-oth-
her)
For you, and take
Your— Hold you go down
You're a ways that long logging
Cinch fried makeshift from which
There's no— No, there's— *Christ* (S-O-U-L),
Help! These words have been on my tongue so long
They're mangled and broken. Once they were song.

21

To wake in the morning to no light.
A sound of birds outside the wall.
Birds, birds, if I knock on the world
Will you listen? Carole? Are you there?
Or as far off as Bill and Anna, walking
The flat plain of the day's breaking stage?

I've burned up my best words in prose.

And now the night burns down its trees.
Turn back, run, it's all over, unless
You let me
Burn again between your knees.

FOUR

22

A crow's cry,
Bare branches on a black tree. November sky.
Evasive speech.

The wind's drone.
See the meadow sway its brown and gray bones
With it. Blown seeds.

First snow.
Those padded tracks encircle the cabin, now home;
Here I go chop wood.

Ice. Icicles,
Sticks of ice, stalactites like long teeth, trickles
From heat. Go cookstove.

See these teeth,
Clenched, aching, unstrung along their edges, bit to keep
From spreading in cold

The word about
Our precarious life like you do, infant in arms, dear daughter,
With wide-open mouth.

23

January; these gray, pragmatic, task-
Filled days, when I'm drawn from you by
Figures and figurines, idolatry of inner speech,
And fantasies not worth the breath to talk about,
And a penny on the heart weighs more than married love.

24

I stared the stars in the face for an answer
And the moon appeared—it was no apparition,
The gold round host
In a cold sky.
It spoke:
Dark is nearer my heart than light;
I arrived, as you, out of equal circumstance,
And I, as you, reveal myself at night.
You see death has taken my face
And ages before the rest but my eye
Looking down wondering why you tremble
When you contend only with her or a her and I
With the irresuscitability of myself,
Myself, myself, and this— ambiguous sky.

25

We've all played games, I guess, and all indulged in tosses
Of the dice. Well, I won the contest, once, but not without losses.

Carrying torchlight down the axe-handled hall,
Bearing my trophy of remorse,
I creak slow in this dream of dread—
Bloated cattle in the passageway, the ghosts
Of dead beasts at my back;

Then the sequence changes:
There's a sloping plain with a spiral
Staircase leading downward,
And I enter my realm and step
By step descend into the rest of the Vikings.

26

The moon goes hollow in the night,
A hole to pass through;
Tail ends of stars lie over our bed and my eyelids,
Stones in pastures,
Relatives under graveyards of grass, an Indian's skull
Sunk in a mound,
The bones of a horse, bleached and in full gallop on a
Hillside—

I turn to you, then turn the knob and turn to the sky,
And next to Orion the stars are startled to see this
Black horse come through the moon's dark half,
Flanks flecked with flying saliva and foam,
And begin to gain on its hillside tilt,
Turning into your interior truth.

27

I see myself in the coffeepot,
The back yard about me in a bulge
After breakfast, which travels wide;
The chromium sphere holds sky and
Foliage along its sides
Like continent and sea.
My features swim there, Valerie.

Beyond the clutter of dishes and cameras,
Perennials, unidentified as yet,
The swimming pool, clean, haunted, three apple trees,
And, after a fall of lawn, the stone gazebo,
Tangled second growth,
Then the Hudson,
Where orange peels and oil drift toward an unspecific sea.

Above, maples and a hickory,
Stone walls on either hand, boulders due
To be retucked, the gray grape arbor starting to give,
And my face there in the coffeepot, broke
For Eastern, steel flat, fattened,
Hydrocephalic,
Adrift over this alien land.

28

Her hair no longer
Hangs as long;
Adolescence is gone
From her maidenhood
And high frame;
She's an echo of a character
She once saw herself in a mirror as— *Where?*

Cars sigh past
On the Beltline highway
And the descending silence
Unfolds eyes in the air;
Either nothing exists
Other than brick, still,
Or else I'm an echo
Of an echo of all of these cars going,
And there's no one there to hear yet.

The tennis ball whacks
A fretwork, Rick;
The borderliners harp and hymn, and hum
Out a broadcast of
A cockfight down
In Mid or Central America: Echo,

O Echo, are you there, bird,
You who left right—
In morning prayer, Lord God, Father,
Alterer of Life, my Protectorate, Light, and my Creator,
In Morning Prayer.

FIVE

29

Child, parents, peace, death, you
Have deserted me;
There's nothing left but to be myself,
Which is what uproots overgrown birch trees.

30

Let it be, let it be, the stereo needle says inside my ear.
On the days when I most believe I believe that that's true.
Each week I work harder and become lesser in what I let be,
Or larger, depending upon the way I'm picturing me. Now,
With this record playing, I think, Yes, Yes, *Do* . . .
But will what I'm saying Yes to be the same tomorrow if I
Let it? How the record revolves is a bound and reliable
Aspect to me. It ends,
Once removed, by use, at the least, its quotidian degree,
Then the straight jacket, lock and key,
Music being a way of being myself without flesh, besides
Being what it is autonomously, assuming no
One had formed it in a circle and said, Let it be:
Whisper. No joy. No shout. The faded words have
Dimmed and now come raggedly out: Let it be you and me.

31

Oh, I haven't fed the chickens for six days,
The record keeps spinning *Aïda* around.
The stately jug on the kitchen table keeps
Smiling back, and is about half brown.

Should I kill the bitch in a dozen slugs,
Or wring a chicken's neck for my next meal,
Or walk above to the hospital again and hear
Her labored breath, that sucking machine,

Or unnail my bedroom window, and set the old
Record player up in it, now that it's spring,
Days double-minded and unstable in every way,
And go out to our garden and break ground?

32

Tonight if I had in me nine-tenths of my life, I'd
Get up on this barstool and I'd dive on a knife.
Oh, it helps to— *Haw!* Oh, I've offended my
Friends and my family, too, with my brag
And nastiness, performed after two
A.M. over long-distance lines.

It helps to be oiled to be honest, Bub.
Bring me another drink.

When I'm drinking I don't like to wash,
And that's the lobster you smell,
And if you don't like it, lady,
Then you and your nose can both go to hell.

Oh, it helps to be oiled to be honest, yes,
Bring me another drink.

Once at a party on Sutton Place
I bumped a big canvas off of a wall
And told the hostess what I thought of her face,
Well, my flying coat tackled me in the elevator hall.

Oh, I've shouted so loud children have shivered!

I've sung so off-key *I* was ashamed!
I've lied about my marriageable status,
My income, my age, my business, my name!

I've spilled drinks and broken glasses,
Passed out on the floor all night
And pissed it, dropped hot ash over her dresses
And been helped by her in unsuccessful fights.

    Oh, it *pays* to be oiled to be honest!
    Bring me another drink!

Last night I kicked her in the ribs and on a run
Blew my cookies down the dishes in the sink,
Seeing in Technicolor rushes what I'd become,
Or was to her, a walking-talking Spiritual Stink.

I have to be oiled to be honest,
So bring me another drink, please,
As I close this on this rainy day in
This roadside bar up north of Kalamazoo,
By apprising you all, family and ex-friends,
Of how I'm about as happy with me as you. *Amen.*

33

I am an almost empty cage.
  The only animal
Left to me is a mistreated panther,
  In a rage,

Who's moved watchers of pure stone
  By her persistence
To live or die in blamelessness on a diet
  Of shadows of bone.

Is there greed in beasts,
  And does the greed
Extend to human greed if the beast's near death?
  Do you sense the *triste*,

Panther, that philosophers ascribe to you?
  Can we reunite
What remains of containment and is dying wild
  In this Zoo?

34

Hand me down that golden mask, Jerome, my silver-headed
Cane and turquoise rings. I'm tired of this act.
Selflessness and piety come in even tides,
Unbiblical Christianity broke my back.
From Quasimodo to Larry Olivier, come!
Hand me that jug and those elephant-skin gloves and that silk hat
And then hand me the hat rack!
I'm going to strut down Fifth
Like a *hi*-y'all-yella jiveass,
Carrying passing-by fox
Fur off on my coat hooks,
Boomalay, Boom,
Hand me that mask!

35

Head bowed, staring down at
A blurred and monstrous ERT:

Typewriter keys. Did sleep eat thought?
Eaten thoughts have made me pull out hair
And itch, tripped my heart into tachycardia,
Reacquainted me with breathing in a dog pant—
Sticky teeth taste green—
And typing them has muscled my back with tin.

Have I also done this? Stabbed my
Thigh with a pencil point? The blaze
Around the puncture wound's bigger than a bee
Sting, like that immovable cyst whose membranous
Blister forms in my brain with no rest, overspread
With spiky filaments like the hairs on human moles, bleached.

Could I create this sort of swelling on paper if I stabbed
It? I stab it and the period bell bursts open in broken rings.

SIX

36

A foreign piece carved out by sleep,
An unclassifiable gleam, a person I've
Never met inhabiting my eyes
When I dare look, intoxicating my depths—
This I wake to, in Him my walking wake begins.

37

The white face beyond the window
    Is only
Your reflection, daughter, and not a ghost
    Here to close
Our eyelids down. Not that again now. No.

    (Remember how I carried you,
    Cradled between my thighs
    For twenty-six years?)

All the same, the sight of it plain
    As grace
Has made my flight stop, believing I saw,
    Caught in that pane,
My developing face at exactly your stage.

38

When I'm drawn at last to last judgment
To give my account of this and the rest,
The treading of others to get it here,
The kite tail of sin keeping it true
To the winds of change and its "inner
Truth," knowing my tongue itself has roots
In hell, unable to evade, revise,
Put off, or change appeal, the reams
Sealed and sewn seven times seven through
Their spines, the tapes of my hopes for it
And every imagination of
My heart at creative zero also
At hand, incorruptible, will I be
Weaving night clouds and the practical,
As before, as now, through eternity,
A word- and worm-scattering warrior,
Your father and protector too few years,
A bullet-shaped helmet of polished
Tin gripping my salvaged skull; and will
It, too, melt down to ink and a type-
Face, a common or noble, readable one,
This one, or one that might meet pure white
In a phrase and one day pass, perhaps,
Across a page under your eyes,
Open to the sun: *I'm alive . . .*

39

The glacier stares its azure stare
And those gleams are a hint of the flood.
When will this spring's weighty stage melt,
And grind me driving in the pocket of her blood?

After grief, peace comes. The bones in their
Sheaths of flesh no longer ache or cut.
Sleep comes; comes, comes,
And fills your pocket up.

40

When I woke, the dam had burst,
Water was flooding the fields
Where grain rose in green spikes
And raying beards that swayed
Forward with the current's strength,
And I was pulled from the pit and wrote:
How long has it been since I've spoken?
I want to say that our hill is overlaid with snow,
That its trees are, that spring is close, and that
Love awoke in me and Love awoke.

41

The rain falling for two days,
And across the lake the sheets of light
Falling between the rain.
"Flowers pop up!" you say as a two-year-old, a line
From a scriptural book your great-grandmother sent
From Oregon, kind Grandma.

And the leeks do.
They've grown three inches with all this rain,
All this light borrowed from one half of the moon;
They grow at night, like you and I do,
Stretching under covers
To reach our real height,
Hearing the rain, the rain for two days,
And seeing between leeks and sheets and waves
Of it, and past the laughter from your upside-down
Face between your legs, all this lightning and light
And then your light, little one. I can make out our
Lineaments and flaws full-face in it, and I'm not
As afraid as I used to be in the night.

42

Help me celebrate what's made without remission,
As though it were stones broken, brickwork
Laid, metal hammered on a blank-faced anvil,
The diverging paths in the fields leading neither
Right nor left nor wrong but where I chose—
Was chosen to go, toward the inland oblivions of song.

SEVEN

43

This leaf that lies lengthwise in light
Across needles of pine,
Lifting its edges toward light,
Dead, half dead,

Dying,
Detached from its source
As I am,
Is gold-red and lies flat.

It curls,
Edges bending to touch one another as at birth,
When it was silver-green,
Downed with silver hair, unfurling, in—

Was that in April? *That* April? In these woods? *Where?*
There are streaks of light along the leaf and darkness around,
And I don't move out of fear of death,
Which is there.

It curls more.
I lie down,
Drawn beyond my need to judge
Nature and others,

Now at least, at last,
And relax around this leaf,
Alone in my past,
And listen to the blowing rumors it repeats of myself.

They are not that bad ...
Except, if I've ever really
Harmed the honey-lined hive
Of my homebound love, dear you.

44

The straight-falling snow,
The balsam we cut from below
The bluff bushy on the banquet table,
The amber lights above the fireplace
Ablaze, the boughs you wove
Reddening on the wall, the vows
And oaths we swore, not to ourselves—
Let those be—but the source and first
Celebrant of second Adam's Eve,
Earthbound and boundless,
Provider of fire, air, fields of snow, and poetry,
Christ, O Holy Spirit, within the Word walking
Within God.

45

Words born in the mind,
Scenes of confusion,
Letters bent like bent wire,
Barbed,
Battles to be fought,
Hackles smoothed,
Thorns combed out,
Then laid in a line.
Tears to confuse you,
A gun at the ear;
The battle,
The war never done.

A scene for you. Scene
Of confusion. Words.
Born. Mine. Each a
Cell on a page,
Then worn to
Cilia roots
By fingers eyes mouths
By you.
Thank you.

46

Bill Livingston,
Dead in his workshop-warehouse, where
He designed and hand-built sailboats of every size
To his ingenious mechanics, all still skating on
The Great Lakes, or off Florida, or farther off,
And slept at his desk chair or on the deck
Of the one he was finishing up,
To the sound of the bay, where he bathed and shaved,
Outside the big gray shed's back doors that rolled, beyond
The rust-stained tub with lion-claw legs he built fires
Under to melt down lead for ballasting his keels,
On a winter night when the bay was ice,
Dead under the moon.

※

The big round stove, like a boiler from
A ferry fired with birch and ash and oak,
Going on beyond the tender's watch of it, most likely,
The shifting air seeking its separate state of perfect heat,
The cases of collected moths on the raw fir bookshelves
Looking out in mid-flight from behind glass bordered with tape
In the direction of this less meticulous pinning,
But as sudden as theirs,
A clot in the brain.

No visitors that night,
None of the philosophers, cracker-barrel or not, feet up,
Dreaming down the line of the boiler's even heat, none
Of the transients, hunters, tradesmen, not one of the young
Drawn like the boats you brought into being, new each spring,
Then released; not, till later, Elizabeth, your wife, rising
From sleep at the cold unraveling inside like broken speech;
The new C— nearly done, the coffee and tools unplugged,
The stars of that changing northern port the same as the holes
In the roof overhead, your hands that could have been cast in
Bronze closed on a tool that none of us here
Expected you to use.

✻

Paternally fretting
About your daughter,
Twenty-three and unmarried,
And the two others on their way up,
Reading botanical texts and Matthiessen and Camus and Mowat
At the desk chair
In those off-hours when nobody can work,
Including craftsmen in love with craftsmanship,
The whirr and eternally altering, alternating blade of the planer,

Those spars and ribs of a brook you wanted to breathe;
Given a big spread that spring in *The National Observer*, you said,
"I maintain there is no sin in being idle," and got taken seriously.

＊

Elizabeth,
I'm not to jib
At this and now head it toward you
And Bill Jr., and two of the three
Daughters I've presumed into my bight;
It's nearly all I've made over the new year,
My "I" dying inside a wide and vast silence.
Our past-midnight talks might be different now;
I wouldn't bring along my six-pack of distractions;
I've packed away the clothes I wore
Playing Martyr in my popish way
For those who ought to be Popes;
My consuming need for affection
Is giving way to my daughter's needs
And I'm ready to let her and the elderly
Enjoy childhood without envying them,
And lately see myself, or find myself,
Down on my knees, a latent nuncio
Praying, Please, Lord, oh, *please*.

*

There are gulls here, too, where I rig this up,
On this farther northern shore not quite American,
Namakan,
And stars of every shade of light you can see clear.
Our picnic here would be on a rock island
Sodded with needles,
Wake-em-up's, maybe,
And then he'd row out alone in a lifeboat,
An eagle feather in the rolled brim of his watch cap,
To the *Witchcraft* rocking endlessly in sunlight,
And she and the *C*—— he left unfinished for us
Would as we followed cant and tack easily in and out of all of
These fir-and-cedar fragrant islands of this calm, uncultivated green
Region, toward the true wilderness where we all sail in to sleep.

47

After a long night, the death of sorrow,
The beast dried and clotted on the floor;
A night of lakes, of dreams that drifted into pools and widened,
Spilling over the world's edge
As over an oilcloth map
To fall nowhere,
The sea itself
Leaving,
Plummeting into the fuming pit of fear, geography-wise,
Drawing unbinding flesh, brains,
And unnamed membranous
Uncoiling entities
After it.
          Now I light a cigarette, test
My flesh, partly there,
Reach for the beer bottle on the windowsill,
The funereal fever of alcohol idling wormlike
Over my cheeks; then let go, drop the cigarette
With a stutter into it and push up, a Russian colossus
In a sound like surf from the sheets, free high above long
Fingers, rose-pink skin, frail lids, pale fringe, your wavy
Cascade of hair plaited with morning light across our plain bed,
And know if I could narrow in on you in this precarious state
Without changing my mind or a muscle,

Oh, passed through your prism,
White-rainy lady of the lakes,
I might be a constant, unbroken rainbow.

48

Falling asleep, head folded
On the typewriter top,
Afraid I'll never finish up, I hear footsteps
And she enters this room of that dream, or me
With all her body's wetness;

She came with water this morning, water
And watercress from the spring, and when
I watched her come, the gray-yellow grain,
Clashing under the sun, repeated her name
And nomenclature in a beady running accolade;

There's been a familiar sighing in these
Phrases, too, furrows, whistle-tone below
The flute, a likelihood of life, and I know
One song with wheat-colored notes will rise above
Ground and sway toward my upright wife. No trumpet. No drum.

The wind sprang upon the window at even tide (three violins keep time)
And brought her name full circle and tied it (finger cymbals) to rhyme;
The sheaves lay down and shed their seeds scented with timothy and

                                                  thyme,

And no ribbed clouds above lowered to make the memory of eleven

                                             years malign,

As sheathed in her sheaves of movement she moves me and these through
time,
Pours water over lips, tears sheets of paper and tears sheets, applies rhyme,
And shakes my head up against the hard dies of the confined but
unconfining Sublime.

49

A drink,
A drink, now,
Now I need a drink
Or sedative to help haze her
Eyes and gold hair and what they
Do to me. Red wine, Lord, a last one, pray,
Like that spring of heartbreak on my tongue,
Blood's salt bond beyond the broken fences, the fields
Gone to weed, the deserted buildings' tilt in the snow,
Unused grain decaying in an old den, pestilential silence,
Too, and the resignation of never again being young, again:

To the greater glory of God! To the long
And peaceful sleep of our fathers! To song!
Wind, wheat, washerwoman, Walkyrie, Winchester,
Whistle-stop waitress in western Wyoming, won when
The wild mares and fillies whinnied up out of the wash
Along the winding road; wise warbler, warrior, whetstone,
Thus wild wodawoda awash in waxen woody, awild he, whallering,
Winna thou wanderest wide from wan, and winna thou wanderest wide,
My wife, watch to our wee ones, what our twining has wrought. Cheers!

What painted shape
Have I painted
Myself in,
And what
About the shapes I
Left out?
The round poem with
Earthquakes
And equators
Across it,
Or the flat
One
With a door at
The top?
The litany and
Those
Match heads?
Is this corrupt,
Crap,
Gold for you,
"Not fair,"
Carole,
Or merely a beading of whims?

Bright bird,
Rainy-lady,
Wife,
The book
Of them's
Burned up,
Done,
The logs
Dreaming
Between
Rails
Where the train
Has passed
Thundering,
Now the
Knock
To wake
Coming round the —
Just this under the
Last tie, threshold, this:

I love our everlastingly interleaved
Lives predestined and reinstated by
The Word.